B E A R
POSTCARD COLLECTION
Random House Illustrators' Art

Random House Illustrators' Art

LONDON SYDNEY AUCKLAND JOHANNESBURG

Cover illustration by Maggie Glen

RANDOM HOUSE ILLUSTRATORS' ART

First published in 1993

1 3 5 7 10 8 6 4 2

Copyright © text and layout Hutchinson Children's Books 1993
Illustrations in this edition © the artists 1993

First published in the United Kingdom in 1993 by
Hutchinson Children's Books,
Random House, 20 Vauxhall Bridge Road,
London SW1V 2SA

Random House Australia (Pty) Limited
20 Alfred Street, Milsons Point, Sydney,
New South Wales 2061, Australia

Random House New Zealand Limited
18 Poland Road, Glenfield,
Auckland 10, New Zealand

Random House South Africa (Pty) Limited
PO Box 337, Bergvlei, South Africa

Random House UK Limited Reg. No. 954009

ISBN 0 09 176200 6
Printed in China

RANDOM
HOUSE
ILLUSTRATORS'
ART

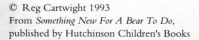

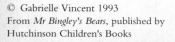

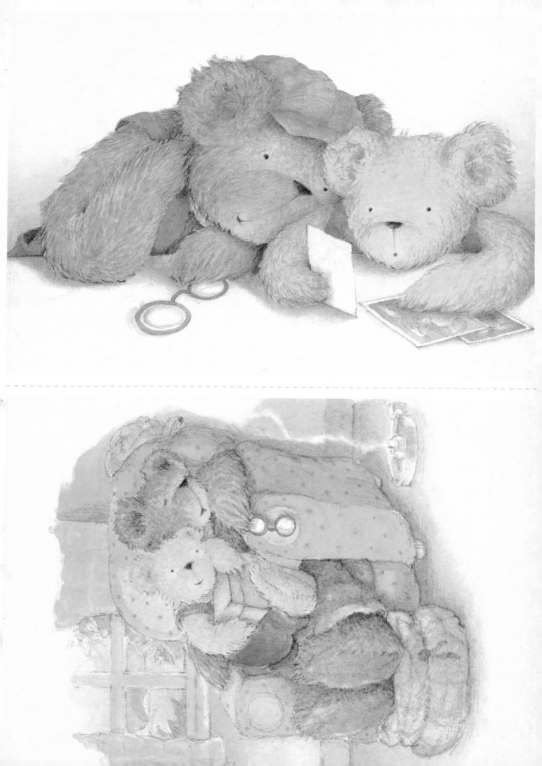

RANDOM
HOUSE
ILLUSTRATORS'
ART

© Peter Bowman 1993
From *Grandpa Bodley and the Photographs*,
published by Hutchinson Children's Books

RANDOM
HOUSE
ILLUSTRATORS'
ART

© Peter Bowman 1993
From *Grandpa Bodley and the Photographs*,
published by Hutchinson Children's Books

RANDOM
HOUSE
ILLUSTRATORS'
ART

© Ben Blathwayt 1991
From *Bear in the Air*, published by
Julia MacRae Books

RANDOM
HOUSE
ILLUSTRATORS'
ART

© Ben Blathwayt 1991
From *Bear in the Air*, published by
Julia MacRae Books

RANDOM
HOUSE
ILLUSTRATORS'
ART

© Maggie Glen 1990
From *Ruby*, published by Hutchinson
Children's Books

RANDOM
HOUSE
ILLUSTRATORS'
ART

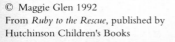

© Maggie Glen 1992
From *Ruby to the Rescue*, published by
Hutchinson Children's Books

RANDOM
HOUSE
ILLUSTRATORS'
ART

RANDOM
HOUSE
ILLUSTRATORS'
ART

RANDOM
HOUSE
ILLUSTRATORS'
ART

RANDOM
HOUSE
ILLUSTRATORS'
ART

RANDOM
HOUSE
ILLUSTRATORS'
ART

RANDOM
HOUSE
ILLUSTRATORS'
ART